Tree Hugging Wild Chimes Book Two

Natasha Georgina Faiers

BookLeaf Publishing

Tree Hugging Wild Chimes Book Two ©
2023 Natasha Georgina Faiers

All rights reserved.

Presentation by *BookLeaf Publishing*

Web: www.bookleafpub.com

E-mail: info@bookleafpub.com

ISBN: 9789395969956

First edition 2023

DEDICATION

To the wild, The melody and warmth. To the wood,
the weather, To the stream the river, To the sun and

rain, Of rainbow panes and of late night stars and
my boots...

My boots soggy and growing something like Jazzy
zinnias crossed with ox-eyed daisies they're

retirement my muddy wellies is one of great
memories. Recycled into pollination growing wild
seeds.

With thanks to every lark and sail. With thanks to
The Wildlife Trusts of whom I was recruited to after

much enjoyed leisure pursuits both as an employee
and as volunteer.

To The Woodland Trust for encouraging and
enabling me to be part of the Tree Stories for woods
and

trees in both 2015 and 2016.

To The English Heritage for the fine adventures and
engagement with historical and to the National

Trust for the many places of interest especially
Constable Country.

To my incredible tutors for lectures and to all the churches of each visit which brought me comfort,

inspiration and solace.

To the wild exploration of waterways and the back waters of the Thames path, the river Roach, The river

Crouch, the lochs and wields and the experiences of those creatures from butterflies to dormouse.

To engagement with falcons of which the leather and lace of tasselled wings was an incredibly beautiful

experience.

To Swan Rescue for doing such incredible work.

To the arts houses, museums and libraries which have such a special super quantity of adventures. May

our humble pages greet you with gratitude and healing.

To memories and to adventure.

To all we have missed from sight hounds to book club chats. So many special thanks too to The RNLI

Lifeboats and to the Kent Air Ambulance to which do so much for those adventurous occasionally in

peril.

Thank you!

With fondness & adoration.

ACKNOWLEDGEMENT

Something in particular we highlight is that as an author Natasha Georgina Faiers is reasserting her maiden name.

*Please note some works were published in Essex Belongs To Us in 2017 formerly Natasha Georgina Barrell her marital name.
*Much of Natasha's work has been previously published under the imprints of Remus House also of which reasserting of authorship is deemed to go forward as now by Natasha Georgina Faiers.
Those publications under the banners of Anchor books, Spotlights, Triumph House, Womens Words between 1998 and 2019 are limited editions and any previous published work is of separate project works to this collection of poetry.
This collection is a standing collection published in the full entirety of the aforementioned publications before only as individual verses.
This book brings those works together as pages of its own merits as a wide collection of those she has published previously.

PREFACE

It is a small expression of memories, research of historical and recreational escape to the wildlife, the landscape and the wetlands of three counties. It predominantly is about Essex county yet fleetingly visits to Natasha's place of birth in Kent and through parts of East Anglia and the outskirts of the Thames estuary where her family background has her looking a little at ancestry through her personal verses.

Fox Love

Eight little paws in the foggy grass played,
Under the chenille nights sequin display.
Two furry coal tinted ears appeared,
Liquorice noses sniffing the misty atmosphere.
As hungry golden eyes twinkling shined,
Two fluffy white tipped tails entwined.
A serenade to a velvet night;
Cosy howls in the darks starlight,
Courting lovers enjoying the moonlight.

Damson Moon Love

Moon hangs low in a damson breeze;
Inky light writes loves dappled night.
Stars echo distant memories;
Moon hangs low in a damson breeze.
Owls call out from the singing trees;
Two monochrome hare's pillow fight.
Moon hangs low in a damson breeze;
Inky light writes loves dappled night.

In Broken Dreams

In broken dreams the sweetness flows;
Windfall fruits lay in orchards low.
Brown sugared kisses eager sun;
Baked bronzen as a currant bun.
Rising with warmth like kneaded dough;
Sustenance brings with it a glow.
Late cuddles with amaretto;
Coffee heart to hearts loving fun.
In broken dreams,
Affections recipe it knows;
Mindful love its tenderness sows.
Feeding sense and selves special one;
Attraction drank and fed, well done.
The blending in loves ripeness grows;
In broken dreams.

To Dream Again

The serene skylight,
Its wispy cotton tails and fluff...
Landed lightly, calcite butterfly,
With wings that tinge a match to the hues above.
Then softly in the leaf that drapes its shade,
In friendly tones smiling, mints, limes and sage.
Hello, Hello the blackbirds call,
As soars on fine spread wings a gull...
For the glow that sits in an almost perfect sky,
Warm, gentle, bright and high.
For as days of summer are meant,
My heart sits tonight content.
Blessed the honey haze that came with its shades
of marmalade.
For whispers crept in called my brain...
To far off shores and winding lanes,
To dream my love,
To dream again.

First Light

The dawn leapt in flowers,
Sun-drenched and silken.
The vast mountains shining;
Like a treacle caramel tumbling brandy sauce.
Where hare-clover forever kisses sweet Timothy,
Misted magenta and watermelon,
Foggy hot pinks and fuchsia,
The meadow calling out the sun.
Blushing lime pink grapefruit twisting tangerine beams,
The springs serenade whooshing clarity;
Pure, clear and fluted.
Enchanted within a wild grove,
Sparkling on;
Glistening, gleaming,
Its elegance charming.
Sophisticated; a real classic beauty curves on,
Like a ballet deer love to prance.
The essence of nature's true heart,
See how the sun likes to dance.

Where The Wild Things Play

Just this morning the heart found comfort in a memory,
Or was it just a dream?
Though each balcony flower today has its own gleam.
How we travelled with the light of the moon.
The red vixen led carriage,
The old fashioned roses clinging hitched to the trellis like a
marriage,
Cornflowers blue and calendula too.
The petals open inviting a bride to the sun,
Like some abstract fairy-tale had just begun…
It seemed so real it is true,
Just like a moment of deja' vu.
As the flower pots danced,
Hedgehogs swayed with the plants,
To a tune as young otter played its sweet flute.
A billion gems twinkled the sky,
It was a mildly clear night.
The river sung along as then upon swan wings we flew.
It was a pleasure to dance next to you.
Still the belief strengthened in my heart,
Love in the Middle Ages style,
A courtly gesture full of warm smiles.
Maybe, just maybe the dream was true,
For just last night we travelled with the light of the moon.

Dear Sunflowers

Dear Sunflowers…
From earth rich soil,
By the wayside grow,
Sprouting green stem,
How high can you go?
With happy seeds, ring of fire,
Brightly greet my eyes,
As my feet in passing go.
Nod your head, tell the time.
For which upon festive harvest,
The early evening come and shine.
Sun-riched again delights,
Beyond the farmers stile,
The spheres of hop farm fun.
Pretty petals grow so tall,
Above the yield,
Of sacks of corn.
Sunflower bend your head,
Can you grow as tall as me?
Or reach the eaves of the old potting shed?
Next year again to come,
Golden glory following the sun…

In Ode To Itself

Whatever to believe is belief...

The day started before the dust had even settled from
our dreams.
The wind roaring like the to and through flow of new
season blowing in.
In the garden small drafts of colour, green stems
really protruding ready to burst open. Here I am
cycles of creaking fence posts and stained glass beads
upon windchimes frolic jangling with dappled sun
streams and damp wash of rain on breezes. Blossom
humming recognition in the gentle brush of
conservatory windows.
Piles of ground elder stem recently grouped for the
new shoots of cold soil seeking the warmth of the
balmier days. Draped was the thrown pea canes
shuffled with upside down pots of where just last
Summer.
Into late Autumn the sweetness of the waves of
sweetpeas drew their jewels. Poker dot of butterfly
had been with bee upon the glossed sheaves where
kniphofia and Gladiolus sat.
Emerging slowly and steadily the new world peace,
pheasant eyes. Silverware of iris the pale blue fairies
upon horses backs lamenting;
Stroking galloping wild grassroots.

I have no idea how it could yet by way realistically I
looked up the seed of broken cloud lines drawn in by
passing sun. In a while of moments passing in my
memory the shipping of my mind to wherever it may
be. Its wandering in silhouette gracious,
present, a strong highlight to acknowledge just so
presence. Maybe it was just my imagination turning
around my emotions. Maybe the silly in my hope it
was a possibility.
Maybe it was just the silence becomes visible in the
such-like of no reply.
Or maybe it was all and more and Hello I am with
you all,
I miss you all and I love you all too.

It was what it was and the evolution one turn of the
sunshine and it swept through.
Back to empty cups awaiting tea and hopeful in the
seed it was returning another hello;
Thank you it resembles.

Gentle rhythm peaceful coexistence in a stormers
breeze.
Wind singing again Thank you.
Light passing through to terms of the slender dip into
the height of lagoons blue hue.
Deeper still with its trail of solar, hesitant it twinkling
starlight glows which stronger shone in darker shades
in drop of nocturnal.
The brush of red a nose in the hazel,
hawthorn in bud, berry to be merged in Rowan
antlers and horns of fennel bronzed early.

Things are going to be very different.
Yet in the whole Scape the panaromic;
of the from and to is the honesty in its moon warts.
The freckled face of the skyline in star gazing nodes.
Unknown binding the known. Inner sense, sensitivity
and the specification is healing.
Time is as in its entirety essential. Corner of corner,
circle of circle and route of route.
Even first glance of chance take charge in the energy
and uplifting freedom in the enthusiasm of the
continued efforts to engage. Ensure all is raised, it
balanced with the understanding deeper still. If I am
of you, you of me and so keep going onwards. If it
was a stumbled moment held in a memorable
experience;
no matter how to view the attachment it striving
towards the purpose.
Lovely it feels to know and to acknowledge how I
adore you.

Fallen Leaf

A canary sky hints at vanilla,
A golden goddess rose rolled in gold.
A regal gala draped like a Spartan,
A plum sugar of scarlet kisses stole.
An apricot drizzling in honeycomb,
Juicy as lemon citrus marmalade.
Ripe berries rambling butternut gourds,
Rusty russets rouge blushing jewels.
Drifting in maple, sweet chestnut, wild cherry,
bramleys tumbling in fall.
Daybreak streams blending poppy and bright
marigolds,
A watercolour of sunshine prisms,
An autumnal treasure to behold.

Buttercup Sunshine

In buttercup sunshine mellow;
Burst dandelions warm yellows.
That morning star so bright and bold;
Sing nightingales the sunrise gold.
Sweetly kissing drift wind clocks blow;
Hop first rabbits from their burrow,
Glowing light casts off the shadows.
A new beginning day unfolds;
Buttercup sunshine.
Awakening fresh green meadow;
Winding morrows journey hedgerows.
Choir of birds dawn marigolds;
Friendly chatter the loves of old.
As heralds the day's first cockcrow,
Buttercup sunshine.

Dance Around The Rose Moon

In a dance around the rose moon;
The dreamer's lake was all in bloom.
Perfect cycles reflect the sky;
Upon barn owls wings fairies fly.
Seldom heard the enchanted song;
Floating where the star light belongs.
Silhouettes of those loved and gone;
Mysterious spirit of night,
In a dance around the rose moon.
The night's sunlight fanciful tune;
With elfin shoes we wander too.
Drifting lanterns of the hearts light;
Flickers sparkling in starlit eyes.
Until the sun rise comes so soon;
In a dance around the rose moon.

Hazelwoods Hope

Spherical ball of woven grass,
Mossy branch and branches grasp.
Hold tight the pantry's hazelnuts;
Sleep sweet whilst the deer do rut.
Honeysuckle again will trace;
Awake in April showers bathe.
In the deep wood keep your place;
Love remains in your wood side hut.
Spherical ball of woven grass,
Little creatures live long to last.
Scamper in the light green wood pass,
Crab apple branch small feet do strut.
Dear Dormouse you're now all grown up,
For there lies hope in patchwork hub.

Fairy Love

The little lane sat starlit,
The night was velveteen.
We came upon a fairy circle,
There upon a dream.
The cottage pinks and baby blue wisteria bowed,
They swayed upon the breeze.
The bunnies were content and playful,
The primrose bent to early butterfly.
The gossamer hammocks shimmered,
As the fairies all danced on by.
Fine suited as a fox-glove;
The fairy boy declared his sweetheart with a wish,
Songs of the bluebird filled the early air with a kiss.
The rose she blushed and then with love in their eyes;
They both married in the morning sun and took off to
sunny climbs.

Hope In The Heath

Hopeful journeys woodsman follower;
The ancient heart of the wood wishes you home.
Bluebirds eyes charm the good luck dear travellers;
The wood ant's green fingers the cow wheat have
sown.
Woodpecker knocks and our lady's gloves sing for
you;
Aged oak twirls the coppice new acorns have grown.
Bounce free with the tune of the foxes gliew;
Dance in the dappled shine thrown from the sky.
Dusky wings flit, glide fairy gowns in the dew;
Drifting a painted dance pattern as they flew.
A patch quilted in promise beyond the red clover;
A warm light on heath, leaf reflects butterflies.
New glade in the shade for loves crossed over;
Hopeful journeys woodsman follower.

*Foxes glew or gliew is old English for musical
instrument consisting of bells.

Deeper Than The Oceans

You are so beautiful my love;
A kiss deeper than the oceans.
Dear darling, sweetheart, loving dove,
You are so beautiful my love!
Tenderness, love your cuddly hugs,
The most adored in devotion.
You are so beautiful my love;
A kiss deeper than the oceans.

Beyond Hours

If ever we could capture togetherness;
When lamplight has strayed with stars.
The glow of the day twirling ribbons;
My world spinning with yours.
A musical raven has flown to its heather nest;
Lamb's wool has snuggled to graze.
Owl's wisdom has reached the brooks crest;
The moons wick gleaming its phase.
If ever we could capture togetherness;
When we sing as chattering birds.
Dip our love in the ointment of intellect;
Allow silenced waves to escape with herds.
A faraway look draws us closer;
Each our own chapters guardian doors.
Our lips each a cup kissing pages;
To drink our words for I love you more.
We have become more with each tender hour;
From which our seeds have gathered new dreams.
Tomorrows are mapping forever purely;
Let our loves sunshine smile, say hello and rise again.

Bridging Seasons

There's a bridging in the seasons;
Fresh doorways light, bright, pleasing.
We wander with the changing leaf;
Revolving clouds to us beneath.
Reflect the rivers relations;
Courting feathers sweet liaisons.
Blend the field with corn silk person;
Prance butterflies to pea and sheaf.
There's a bridging in the seasons;
Where the wildflowers trailing run.
A patchwork quilt in peach blossoms;
On clover bank just out of reach.
In harmony hare, cricket leap;
Walking beauty needs no reasons,
There's a bridging in the seasons.

A Wintry Tale

Last night our patch of globe drifted,
Met with sugar whitening.
Pulling on woolly's, ugg boots, big coats,
Gloves and extra lining.
Greeted by a wintry scene,
To visit the Gypsy horses we set out.
To see them in the old field in-between.
Down the road we followed,
Birds feet marking in the snow,
Where the fox had been and rode.
To the forest as we wandered sugared whites.
We hushed soft with our own excitement.
The majesty lifted his crown, groaned.
The entire woodland seemed to echo,
A hundred eyes and waking moans.
As there he stood the most regal,
The Royal coated beyond the throne.

City Steps

Of castles and of cannons,
Of Dickensian costume dress.
The sail makers and the Sergeants Mess.
Of the Guildhall, Penny Farthing,
A street of odd curiosities.
Of Poets Corner, of cathedral chimes,
Tales of battle Kings,
The Rose and Crown and Queen Victorian gowns.
Fagin's Alley, a picnic in The Vines,
For a little wander,
Local history and of memories caught in time.

Passed Times

Passed Times…
As if time reversed and waited,
Liken an hour-glass grains had spent.
The pastures landmarks caught in painted,
For time to show the paths they went.
Old track the chugging locomotive,
It could easily be the eighteenth century.
On a steam railways platform,
The trunks awaiting a journey to the sea…
A long kiss goodbye and the noise of many feet,
Puffing Billy and the last call for a seat.
Voluptuous in petticoats,
Waving handkerchiefs.
The jackets, hats and luggage,
All aboard it's time to go…
For the shadows in a moment of day-gone year,
A step in time to what was then,
Of so long ago.

*Circa 1813 the locomotive Puffing Billy one
example of the style train generations would
journey to
holiday in Margate.

Table Manners

I am waiting perplexed, surreal I feel;
Images of birds of paradise,
Ornately displayed through arches rise.
Delicate brush has feathered on distressed wood;
Tables placed with topiary obscured views.
Consistent chatter, the chink of china;
Reminiscing as I sip.
Busy people are striding, passing;
Searching for a reason to leave the dregs of another
day's toil casting.
Double espresso seems to ponder over;
The article in a discarded newspaper,
Ear marked today's horoscopes and a moon in the
balance.
Looking up to the hills the seasons have mellowed;
A chestnut panettone stretching before me the call of
hiker's boots.
On seeing the waiter in surplus copiously he refills
my cup;
Gratifications and maybe's I tip him small silver.
Amaretti is teasing for I am hungry it looks
appetising;
Then meets eyes at the brim of a fedora;
You're here I suddenly realise gently welcoming.
Now stronger anticipation engulfs;
What starts conversation into some realm of eternity.
Your arrival has captured me like a small bird,
Somersaults my stomach in butterfly wings.

My attention obeys rhythmic like a lost songs
recalling,
Soft lights and mystery my heart longs to place.
Your canvas is an art gallery of exceptional beauty;
Should I reclaim my suit of armour to padlock my
heart?
The lines around your eyes seem to jar windows;
Only ever contemplated in those moments of
innocent whimsy.
The whole lane with a picket fence and scampering
puppies;Damask roses and an iron swing seat in a
cottage garden.
Future or previous depiction the features are
definitely your style.
Babushka dolls in suite each with your essence
brimming;
Your remedy in mindful mediation on how to lace
shoes.
Like a distant dream reading a thunder glass chanced
with its potion;
The finest day we still reach for the parasols just in
case.
Earlier rains have settled reflections;
Storm clouds long gone and love is well placed.
Your hands are a musicians well versed;
Your eyes glisten with something so precious.
Your promises so endearing so prepared;
Let us be living soup spooning etiquette.
I could join you with napkin rings dearly;
You're here is what matters and something tells me
you're well worth the wait.